Science Experiments

Written by James Maclaine,
Lizzie Cope, Rachel Firth and
Darran Stobbart

Illustrated by Petra Baan and Diego Funck

Designed by Lucy Wain,
Jenny Offley and Samuel Gorham

With expert advice from
Dr. Colin Dodd

Welcome to your science lab

Scientists always ask QUESTIONS about the world around them – and they try to find answers by doing EXPERIMENTS. This book will show you how to think like a scientist, with your own science lab at home.

But don't scientists need specialist equipment?

No! You can do all of the experiments with things that are easy to find.

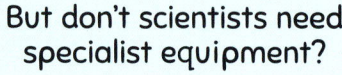

Just read through each experiment before you start it. Make sure you have everything ready and understand what to do.

How can I keep track of my experiments?

Take photos or make videos as you do each one.

It's a good idea to keep a notebook, so you can write down what you see and what you discover.

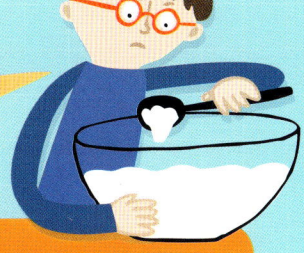

What if an experiment doesn't seem to work?

Do it again!
Scientists often repeat experiments to check their findings and discover even more.

What if I can't work out the answers to any questions?

Don't worry!
There are answers and extra information on pages 59-61.

How do I pick which experiment to do?

You can browse the contents on pages 4-5 or search for a topic in the index on pages 63-64.

Where can I find out even more?

Here's where...

Usborne Quicklinks
For links to websites where you can watch amazing experiments, explore science with online games and activities and find even more ideas for simple experiments to try at home, go to **usborne.com/Quicklinks** and type in the title of this book.

Please follow the internet safety guidelines at Usborne Quicklinks. Children should be supervised online.

Pick your experiment

6   Can you stop gravity?
7   Helicopter seeds
8   What's shocking about static?
10 The look of the Moon
12 Why are seas rising?
14 Seeing strange things
16 Why do bread and cakes rise?
17 Bicarbonate of soda + acid = ?
18 Whose memory is best?
20 The egg that floats and sinks
21 Dancing raisins
22 Can you see sounds?
23 Catching a whisper
24 How do planes fly?
26 In dinosaurs' footsteps
28 Playing with air pressure

Investigate why the Moon is spotty on page 11.

What keeps paper planes gliding through the air?

Follow the steps on page 24 to discover the secrets of flight.

30 Can you really believe your eyes?
32 Transforming pennies
34 Do leaves have skeletons?
35 Why are leaves green?
36 How do insects walk on water?
38 The liquid-solid mixture mystery
40 See inside your hand
42 Why are bubbles round?
44 Forcing things to move
46 Mixing colours without a brush
47 The colours hiding in your pens
48 The secrets of taste
50 Let machines do the work
52 How big is an iceberg?
53 Why don't seals freeze?
54 What makes things balance?
56 How is butter made?
58 Where do clouds come from?
59 Answers
62 Science words
63 Index

I've never seen bubbles of different shapes before. I wonder why not...

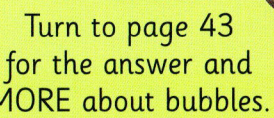

Turn to page 43 for the answer and MORE about bubbles.

What exactly is an iceberg?

You can find out the meaning of ICEBERG and all the science words in this book on page 62.

Can you stop gravity?

GRAVITY is a FORCE that pulls everything down. That's why things fall when they're dropped. But here's a way to slow down gravity's effects with the help of a parachute...

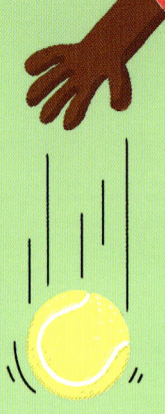

1. Scrunch up two pieces of foil into two small balls, the same size.

2. Tape a piece of string to each corner of a rectangle of thin paper, such as newspaper.

3. Use more tape to stick the ends of the strings to one of the balls.

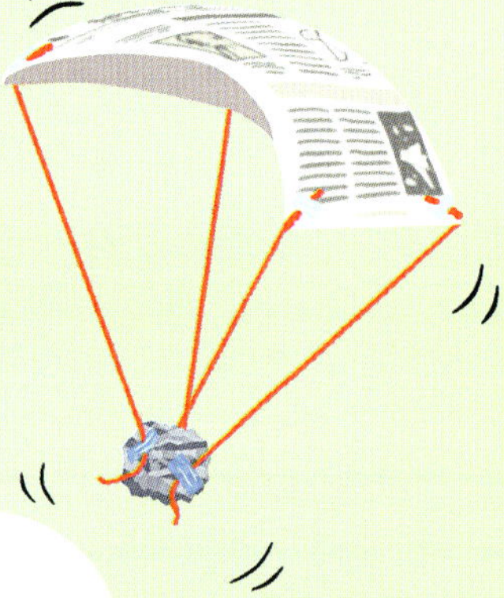

4. Now compare how both balls fall. Drop them from the same height, one after the other.

Spread out the paper parachute before you let go.

You could ask someone to time how long each ball takes to land.

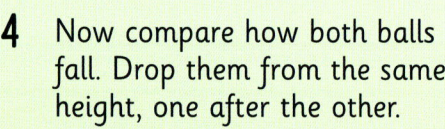

I wonder how it works...

Air trapped underneath the parachute pushes UP against the paper with a force called AIR RESISTANCE. This makes the parachute and ball fall more slowly than a ball on its own.

Gravity can never be stopped, BUT parachutes — as well as falling feathers and leaves — can resist it by trapping air.

Helicopter seeds

Some trees, such as sycamores, spread their seeds in wing-shaped cases. When the seeds fall, they spin like a helicopter and travel further away. To see how they spin, make a mini helicopter and watch it fly.

1 Cut a long strip of paper. Then fold it in half.

2 Fold back both sides, like this.

3 Stick the paper together here.

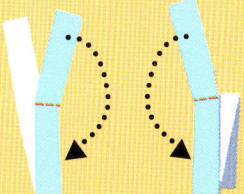

4 Fold along the dotted line to make a wing. Then repeat on the other side.

5 Open the wings.

Push a paper clip onto the bottom.

6 Now hold up your helicopter and let it go.

The helicopter's wings are slanted in opposite directions. As the helicopter falls, air pushes the slanted wings sideways — making the helicopter spin. Sycamore seeds also have pairs of slanted 'wings'. That's why they spin.

But WHY do the seeds need to move away from the tree?

So they have more space to grow into new trees.

What's shocking about static?

If you've ever felt a shock from a door handle made of metal, then you've been zapped by a type of electricity called STATIC.

Ow! What's wrong with that handle?

Maybe there was something on your hand?

Here's the explanation...

BEFORE ZAP!

Shuffling across a carpet causes static electricity to build up in your body...

...and when you touch metal, the static flows into it, giving you a shock.

BUT these next experiments won't hurt – they use a ruler and some tape charged with static instead...

Glue-free sticking

1. Tear thin paper into little pieces. Scatter them on top of a table.

2. Hold a plastic ruler near the pieces to see what happens...

NOTHING!

3. Now rub the ruler on a woolly scarf for about a minute.

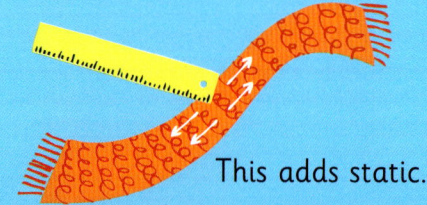

This adds static.

4. Repeat step 2 and watch...

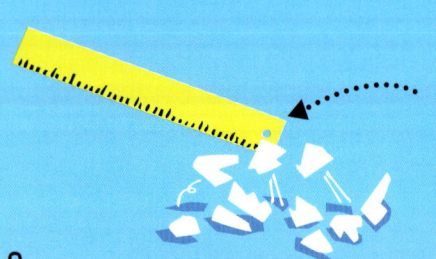

Static electricity ATTRACTS things that don't have any static, like the pieces of paper. That's why they hover and then stick to the ruler.

What result do you expect if you tap the ruler onto metal between steps 3 and 4? Test out your prediction!

Hair-raising static

1 Rub a plastic ruler on a sweater for a minute or so.

Aha. I'm charging it with static.

2 Looking in a mirror, hold the ruler just above your head...

The ruler attracts strands of hair because they have no static.

Bending water

1 Rub the ruler again on a scarf or sweater to build up more static.

2 Gently turn on a tap until a narrow stream of water flows. Then hold the ruler near the water.

Incredible. What's going on?

Because it's attracted towards the ruler, the water bends.

Turn on the tap more. Is the static still strong enough to make the water bend?

Static + static = ?

1 Stick two strips of tape on top of a scarf.

2 Peel off one of the strips. (This adds static to it.) Then stick it to the edge of a table, so it hangs down.

3 Peel off the other strip and bring it near...

If two things both have static electricity, they PUSH each other away.

9

The look of the Moon

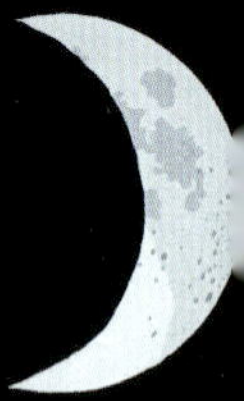

You don't have to visit the Moon to find out some of its secrets. You can study it from Earth by doing experiments instead.

Shape-shifting Moon

The Moon looks as if it changes shape each night. Do this experiment in a dark room with a desk lamp to see why...

Where did the rest of the Moon go?

1. Stand near a light that's a little higher than your head.

2. Push a fork into an orange. Hold it in front of you.

3. Turn in a circle. Can you see a shadow on the orange? Does it change?

Think of your head as the Earth...

...the orange as the Moon...

...and the light as the Sun.

The same side of the Moon always faces Earth – so keep your arm straight and DON'T move the fork.

How the Moon changes

The Moon moves around Earth every month. Different parts of it are lit up by the Sun each day...

 Day 1    Day 5    Day 7    Day 9    Day 14 or 15

Shadow covers the Moon when it's directly between Earth and the Sun.

Then the lit-up part starts to WAX, or grow...

...until you see a full moon.

Why the Moon is spotty

If you looked at the Moon through a telescope, you'd see lots of spots. They're craters, made by space rocks called ASTEROIDS. They slammed into its surface over millions of years.

Dark patches called MARIA can be seen without a telescope. They were left behind when volcanoes on the Moon erupted.

"Why did the asteroids leave these marks?"

"Let's make our own Moon to investigate…"

1. Pour a thick layer of flour into a cake tin.

   (The real Moon is made of rock.)

2. Using a sieve, cover the flour with cocoa powder.

   (The Moon is also covered in powder, called moon dust.)

3. Find a few marbles of different sizes for asteroids. Drop them from different heights.

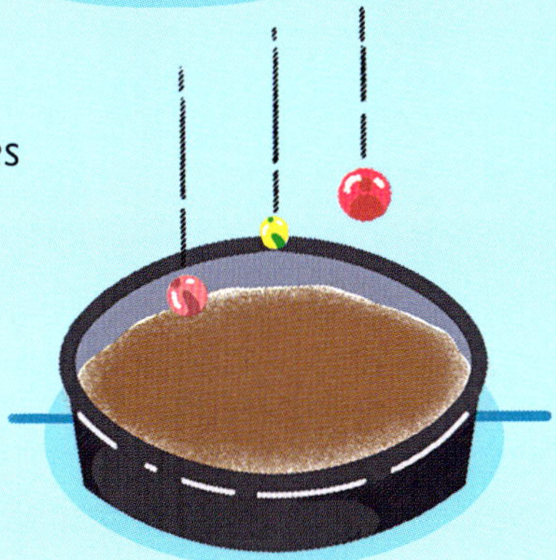

4. Examine your Moon. Which asteroid made the biggest crater?

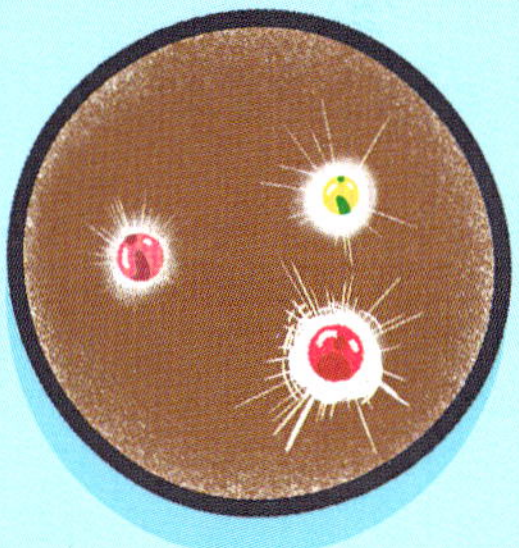

   (This is how asteroids left their mark – by blasting away moon dust.)

Gibbous moon
Day 19

Day 22

Day 25

Crescent moon

Day 30

Over the next two weeks, the Moon seems to shrink, or WANE.

And then the cycle starts all over again…

11

Why are seas rising?

As the world is getting warmer, sea levels are getting higher. This experiment will help you to understand why this is happening – and where all the extra water is coming from.

1. Cut two large potatoes to make their tops and bottoms flat. Put them into two containers of similar sizes.

2. Pour water into both containers. Stop halfway up each potato.

Make sure there's some space.

3. Balance five ice cubes on top of one potato. Then add five ice cubes to the WATER in the other container.

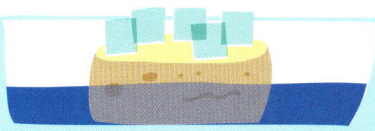 

What's the point of the potatoes, water and ice cubes?

And the ice cubes represent ICE?

Each potato represents LAND on Earth.

YES!
Enormous amounts of ice cover land near the top and bottom of the planet.

And there are huge sheets of floating ice in the northernmost and southernmost seas.

The water is the SEA.

4 Carefully push a pin into the side of each potato to mark both water levels.

 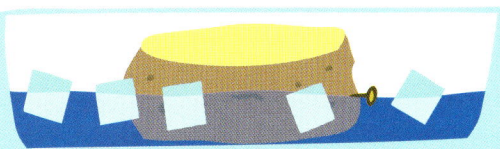

5 Wait until all the ice has melted. Then check the water levels again. What has happened?

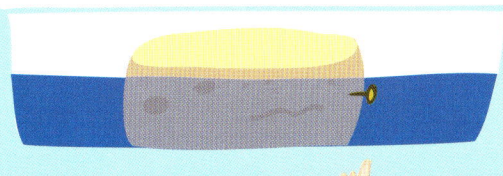 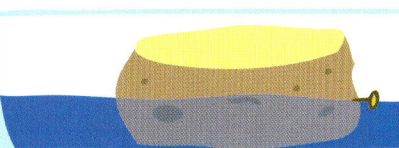

This pin is completely underwater!

The ice has gone BUT the level is still the same.

That's because the water in the ice cubes on the potato flowed into the container.

The ice cubes take up the same amount of space in the container as the water they become. Therefore, the level DOESN'T rise.

So, what's going on in the world?
With hotter temperatures, more ice on land and sea melts each year. BUT it's the melting LAND ice that's running into the seas and making them rise.

Seeing strange things

If you draw pictures on small pieces of paper, you can CHANGE the way they look with the help of a jar and some water.

Magnifying jar

1. Draw two eyes on a strip of paper. They should be roughly the same size.

2. Fill a jar with water. Press the paper against the back of the jar, so you can see one of the eyes through it.

3. Now compare the two eyes. Are they still the same size?

Leave a gap between them.

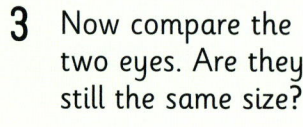

This one looks BIGGER.

Flip the fish

1. Draw a fish, like this.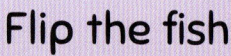

2. Hold the paper behind a jar of water. Look through the jar at the fish.

3. Slowly move the paper away from the jar. What do you notice?

It's swimming the other way!

Vanishing act

1 Copy this rabbit onto a small square of paper. Place an empty jar over the picture.

2 Fill the jar with water. Place it back on top of the picture.

You should be able to see the rabbit underneath.

3 Look through the side of the jar only. Can you still see the rabbit?

Where did it go??

Why do the pictures change?

When you look at ANYTHING, what you're actually seeing is LIGHT bouncing off it into your eyes.

Light usually moves in straight lines, but when it passes between air and water, it BENDS. This is called REFRACTION.

As light bends, it changes the way you see things. That's why the pictures look bigger, flip around or even disappear.

See MORE strange things

Fill jars and glasses of different shapes and sizes with water and then look through them at things, such as...

Patterns   Pictures   Your hand

What unusual effects can you see?

15

Why do bread and cakes rise?

Some cake mixtures contain bicarbonate of soda and some bread recipes include dried yeast. You'll need both these ingredients to find out what they do.

Yeast power

1. Half-fill two glasses with warm water. Stir in a teaspoon of sugar and two tablespoons of strong white flour to each.

2. Stir in a teaspoon of dried yeast to one glass only. Stick a label on this glass.

3. Leave both glasses somewhere warm for 20 minutes. Then check the results.

Who made these frothy bubbles?

The yeast did. It's made up of tiny living things that 'wake up' in warm water. They feed on sugar and flour, producing a GAS called CARBON DIOXIDE, which makes the mixture bubbly. This happens inside bread, causing it to grow.

Soda power

1. Pour hot water into one bowl and cold water into another.

2. Stir a teaspoon of bicarbonate of soda into each bowl. What happens next?

Why is one of them fizzier than the other?

...Because bicarbonate of soda gives off bubbles of carbon dioxide in water when it's HOT.

Can you work out why this matters for cakes? Check your answer at the back of the book.

Bicarbonate of soda + acid = ?

Now discover what happens when you add bicarbonate of soda to ACIDS, such as lemon juice or vinegar.

1 Half-fill a bottle with lemon juice or vinegar. Add a few drops of food dye and squirt in some washing-up liquid. Gently swirl the bottle and place it on a tray.

2 Quickly add a heaped tablespoon of bicarbonate of soda and watch...

When you mix acid and bicarbonate of soda together, they change — or REACT.

This creates lots of bubbles of carbon dioxide...

...which get trapped in the washing-up liquid and food dye, making colourful foam.

Whoa!

How long does it take for your mixture to stop fizzing?

What happens if you add more acid or soda?

Whose memory is best?

Do each of these tests lots of times with as many people as you can. Write down all their scores to compare.

Memory tray

1. Put twelve objects on a tray when no one else is looking. Then cover it with a big cloth.

2. Challenge someone to lift up the cloth, look at the things for 60 seconds and try to remember them all.

3. Cover the tray again. How many of the items can the person write down from memory?

Are numbers trickier to remember?

1. Write twelve different numbers on some paper.

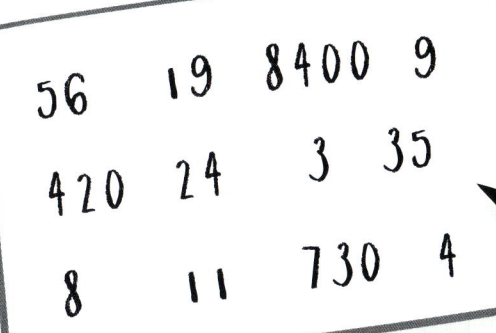

2. Show them to someone for 60 seconds to memorize.

3. Then see how many the person can write down...

Do people make more mistakes with this test? Scientists have found that it's more difficult to remember numbers than objects.

What about words?

1. Repeat the above test with a list of twelve words instead.

tractor
bottle
penguin
cat
Africa
trousers
leg
purple
lamp
phone
train
Sun

Does anyone remember all the words correctly?

2. Then do this test again but tell each person to picture and say the words while memorizing them.

Both picturing things and speaking use different parts of the brain. These extra steps can help people's memories.

The egg that floats and sinks

How can an egg sink and float in the same jar of water? This experiment will show you the answer.

1 Place a fresh egg into a big jar of water.

It should sink to the bottom of the jar. That's because the egg is DENSER (see below) than water.

2 Carefully take out the egg. Then stir in five spoons of salt.

As the salt DISSOLVES in the water, it makes it more dense.

3 Place the egg back in the jar. What does it do this time?

Now the egg should float. If it doesn't, stir in more salt and try again.

What does DENSER mean?

Everything is made up of tiny PARTICLES. The closer together those particles are, the denser something is.

Pick up a piece of dried pasta, and then a coin, to compare how dense they each feel.

Aha!

Next steps

Repeat the experiment with flour instead of salt. Does it mix well? Does it make the egg float?

Then use a pebble instead of an egg. Does the pebble float if you add some salt?

Write down what you find out.

Dancing raisins

What do raisins do if you add them to two glasses of water – one still and one fizzy?

1. Fill the first glass with tap water. Use a new bottle of sparkling water to fill the second.

2. Drop about eight raisins into each glass. Then watch...

Sparkling water contains carbon dioxide. This gas causes lots of bubbles to form. Because gas is less dense than water, the bubbles rise.

At first, the raisins in BOTH glasses sink because they're DENSER than water.

BUT in the second glass, bubbles get stuck to the wrinkly raisins. This makes them less dense, so they float.

At the surface, the bubbles burst. The raisins become denser – and sink once more.

Back at the bottom, bubbles cling to the raisins, which makes them rise again.

Expand the experiment

Do the raisins stop dancing after a while? Why do you think this happens?

Taste the water in the second glass at the start and end. How does it change?

Add smooth things, such as lentils, to a new glass of sparkling water. Do they start dancing?

Can you see sounds?

Sometimes windows shudder and stacks of plates rattle when there are loud noises close by. Have you ever wondered why?

Jumping salt

1. Stretch food wrap over a mixing bowl very tightly. Secure it with an elastic band. Then scatter a pinch of salt on top.

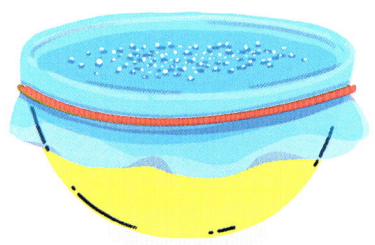

2. Hold a baking tray nearby. Hit it with a spoon until the salt starts to move.

What happens if you hit the tray harder?

3. If you have a speaker, play loud music near the bowl instead. Turn up the volume...

The louder the sound...

...the more the salt moves.

Sound's effects

Sounds are made by fast movements called VIBRATIONS.

Hitting the tray and playing music send vibrations through the air and into the wrap, so it vibrates and the salt JUMPS.

You CAN'T SEE sounds, but you can see salt — or even plates and windows — moving because of them.

Catching a whisper

This simple telephone captures sounds, so you can hear someone whispering from the other side of a room. You'll need two paper cups, two paper clips and some string to make it.

First...

1. Make a hole in each cup by pushing a pencil into the base.
2. Thread a very long piece of string through both holes.
3. Then tie each end to a paper clip.

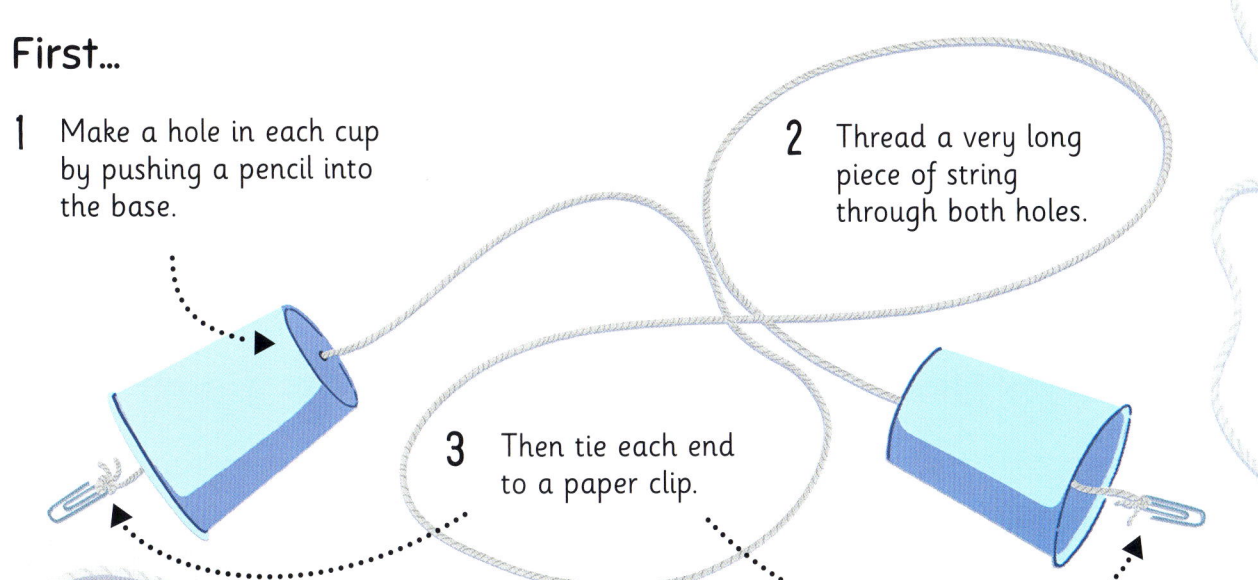

Now test it out...

Ask someone to whisper into a cup.

The little goose likes orange juice.

Hold the other cup to your ear. Can you hear anything?

Keep the string STRAIGHT and TIGHT. Make sure it DOESN'T TOUCH anything else.

How it works

Talking – even whispering – vibrates the air inside the cup. ......▶ The vibrations travel along the string... ......▶ ...into the other cup and then into your ear.

How do planes fly?

Do test flights as you fold a piece of paper into a plane to find out what makes it fly. Remember to note down a description of each flight.

1
Fold the paper in half, like this.

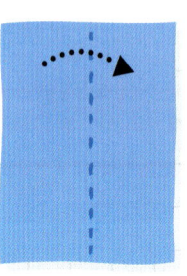

Then hold the folded edge and throw...

First test flight

The folded paper moves forwards...

...but it soon nosedives as the FORCE of GRAVITY pulls it down.

2
Next, open up the paper. Fold down the top corners to the middle.

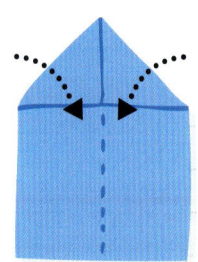

3
Fold both folded edges into the middle.

4
Then fold the plane in half, from right to left.

5
Fold along the dotted line to make a wing. Repeat on the other side.

6
Pull up the wings, so they're flat. Throw it a second time...

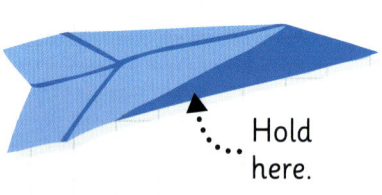

Hold here.

Second test flight

The plane's pointed nose cuts through the air, helping it to flow around the wings. This causes something called LIFT. It keeps the plane up.

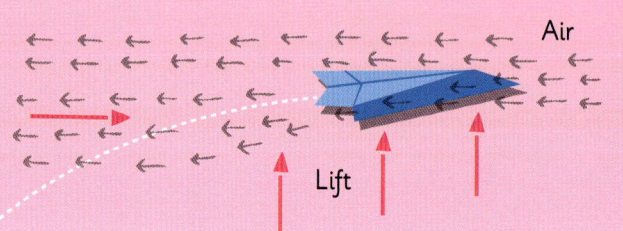

Air

Lift

As the plane slows down, less air flows around its wings. So it loses height and lands.

Now test out the ideas on this page. Check your results with the answers at the back of the book.

Will my plane still fly if I throw it upside down?

Nose clip

Slide a paper clip onto the nose of your plane and then throw it again...

Flight angle

Tilt your plane up or down as you throw it. What effect does this have?

Wing tips

Bend the tips of the wings in different ways before each flight...

Both wing tips UP

Both wing tips DOWN

One UP...

...one DOWN

Only one UP

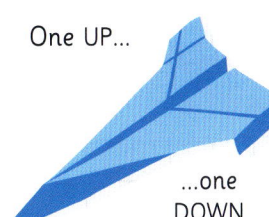

Foil planes and more

Here are some different materials you could turn into planes. Which is easiest to fold – and which makes the plane that flies furthest?

Magazine paper

Cardboard from a cereal box

Foil

If you have a big piece of newspaper, fold it into a jumbo jet. How fast does it fly?

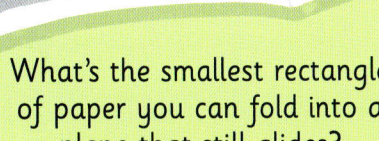

What's the smallest rectangle of paper you can fold into a plane that still glides?

In dinosaurs' footsteps

Dinosaur footprints are sometimes discovered in rocks around the world. They are a type of FOSSIL. You can investigate how they were left behind by making your own prints.

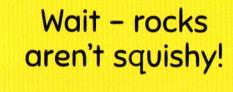
Wait – rocks aren't squishy!

So how did their feet leave these tracks? Hmm...

First mix some salt dough

1. Add one cup of flour, half a cup of salt, half a cup of water and one teaspoon of cooking oil to a bowl.

2. Use your hands to mix everything together. If it feels very sticky, add a little flour.

3. On a floured surface, push and squeeze the dough for about a minute until it feels smooth.

4. Roll the dough flat. Stop when it's about 0.5cm (0.25 inches) thick.

5. Cut out circles with a cookie cutter. Put them on some baking parchment.

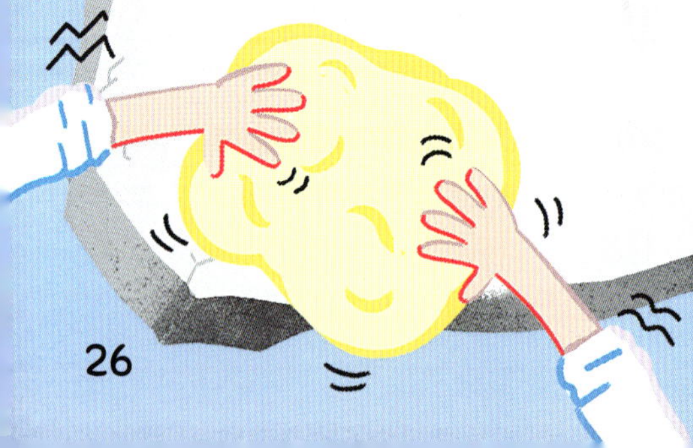

Now print...

1. Pressing the top of a pencil into the dough, make a footprint shape, like this.

2. Leave the prints on a sunny windowsill for about a week.

3. Check the dough every day or two. Does it start to turn hard?

Water in the dough slowly spreads into the air, or EVAPORATES. So the dough gets drier and harder.

From footsteps to footprints to fossils

Dinosaurs didn't walk on salt dough, of course — BUT they did walk on soft mud.

In hot weather, the mud dried out, keeping the shapes of the footprints.

Over a very long time, MORE mud covered the tracks. This extra weight turned the mud underneath into rock.

And when the rock was unearthed, my tracks were seen again.

Playing with air pressure

If you suck water into a straw, cover the top with your thumb and lift up your hand, a force called AIR PRESSURE traps the water inside. See this for yourself before doing these next experiments.

What is air pressure?

Air is made up of lots of tiny particles. You can't see them, but they're always moving and pushing against everything around them. This causes air pressure.

Why doesn't the water fall out?

Air pushes UP into the straw. The pressure is strong enough to stop GRAVITY pulling the water down.

BUT if you remove your thumb, air pushes DOWN into the straw, too, so gravity pulls the water out.

Keeping an upside-down glass full

1. Put a thin piece of card on top of a glass of water.

2. Holding the card in place, turn over the glass. Do this above a sink, just in case.

3. Now let go of the card...

No way!

Air pushes up against the card, sealing it to the glass. The force of the air pushing up is stronger than the weight of the water pushing down, so the water stays in the glass.

What happens if you tug the card?

Underwater paper

1. Scrunch some paper into the bottom of a jar. Turn it over.

2. Slowly push the jar straight down into a bowl of water, below the surface.

Check the paper stays in place.

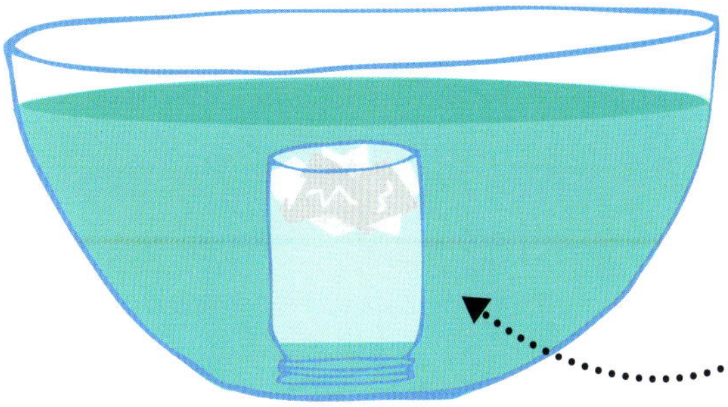

DON'T tilt the jar.

3. After a few seconds, lift the jar straight back up. Then check the paper...

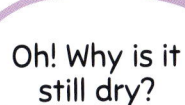

Oh! Why is it still dry?

As you push the jar down, the air pressure inside it is strong enough to push the water away. No water can get in, so the trapped air keeps the paper dry.

Raising the level

1. Push an empty, upside-down jar into a bowl of water. Then tilt the jar, so the air goes out and water flows in.

Why do you think there are bubbles?

2. Carefully lift up the jar. Stop when the rim is just below the surface.

Why is the water level in the jar ABOVE the water in the bowl?

Air pressure pushes down on the water in the bowl, forcing some of it up into the jar.

Where does the water go if you raise the jar higher?

Can you really believe your eyes?

No! These puzzling pictures will trick your eyes and baffle your brain. They're called optical illusions.

Looking longer

Which of these two red lines looks longer? Make your decision before measuring them.

The sloping lines make you think that the red lines are different sizes.

Changing colours

Does one end of the long, thin rectangle below look darker than the other? To check, cover up everything around it with pieces of paper.

The rectangle SEEMS to get lighter because your brain compares it to the other blues.

Which picture?

Is this a picture of a vase... or two faces?

It's VERY hard to see BOTH at once. If you look at the faces, the vase becomes the background — and vice versa.

Ghost shape

Can you see the shape that ISN'T really there at all?

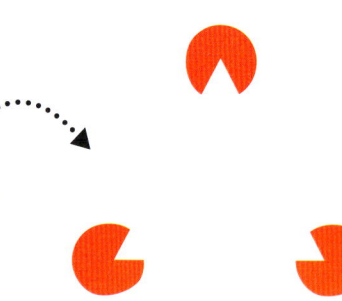

The wedges cut out of the circles help you to turn the space in between into a big triangle.

How do illusions work?

Your brain is good at taking shortcuts. It quickly judges things you see by comparing them to each other. It can even fill in missing details.

Usually, this helps you to make sense of what you're looking at — BUT illusions are designed to trick you.

Make your own optical illusion

1. Draw a large oval on a piece of paper and cut it out.

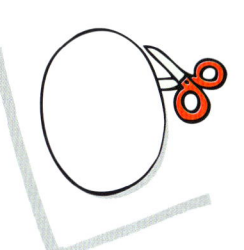

2. Make four cuts into the paper, like this.

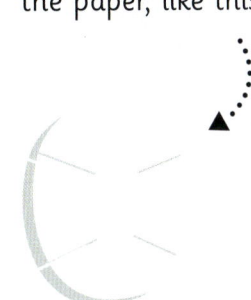

3. Following the arrows, glue one side of each cut over the other, to make a curved mask.

Trim off any pointy bits.

4. Using a black felt-tip pen, draw a face INSIDE the mask, copying this picture.

5. Now stick your mask to a door with poster tack. Look at the face. Do you notice anything strange?

Try covering one eye and stepping forwards and backwards.

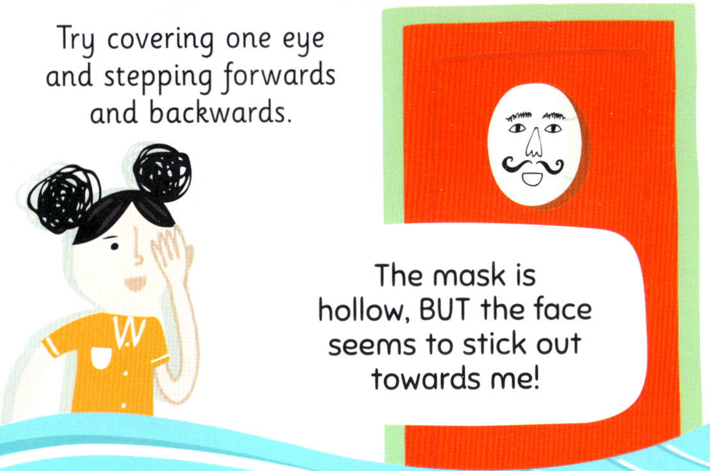

The mask is hollow, BUT the face seems to stick out towards me!

What's going on?
Your brain is used to seeing faces that stick out, so that's what it EXPECTS to see. When you look at the mask, your brain tries to see it as a normal face, even though you know it's hollow.

Do a screen test
Make a video of your mask, moving the camera slowly in front of it, from side to side.

It works even better!

The flat screen makes it HARDER for your brain to tell which way the mask curves.

Transforming pennies

Pennies are coated in copper metal, BUT some pennies look less shiny than others. Discover why – and how to use science to clean them – on these pages.

Why am I darker?

Over time, copper changes, or REACTS, with OXYGEN in the air to make a chemical called COPPER OXIDE. An old penny is mostly covered in copper oxide.

Reshining pennies

1. Put two dark pennies into jars. Pour water over one and vinegar over the other.

2. After ten minutes, remove the coins. Rinse both in water and rub them dry with kitchen paper.

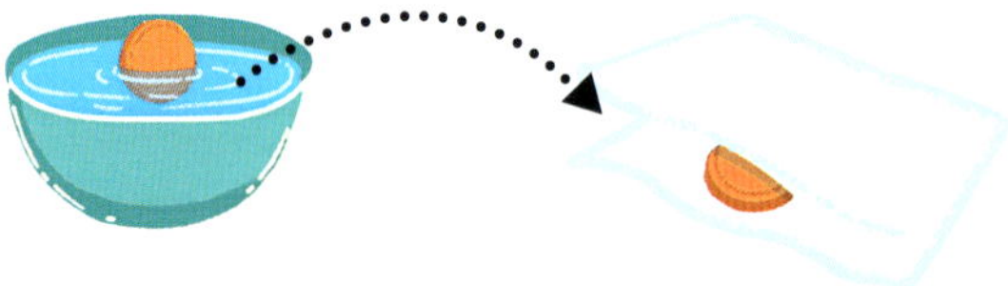

3. Check both coins. What do you see?

Water and paper alone CAN'T clean off copper oxide.

BUT the penny left in vinegar looks MUCH shinier.

So how does vinegar clean coins?

Chemicals called ACIDS break down copper oxide. And because vinegar contains acids, it cleans the coin.

Identifying acids

Find out which liquids contain acids by testing how they clean pennies. Leave pennies in milk, lemon juice, oil or cola. Then compare the results.

Under a statue's skin

Over 130 years ago, the Statue of Liberty in New York City was brown like a penny. That's because it used to be covered in copper.

But the copper reacted with water and gases in the air making a blue-green mixture of chemicals known as VERDIGRIS.

I wonder if the copper is still there...

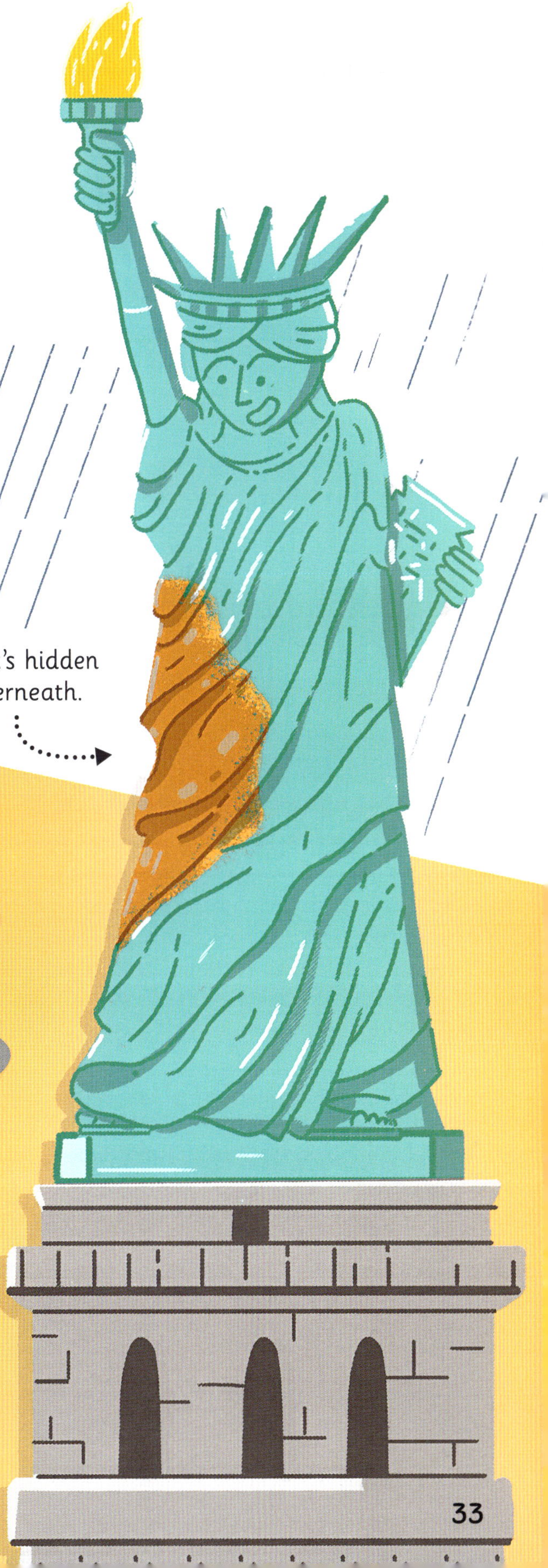

Yes! It's hidden underneath.

Turning pennies blue-green

You can see verdigris form on a penny...

1. Fold kitchen paper in half. Put it on a plate.

2. Soak the paper with vinegar.

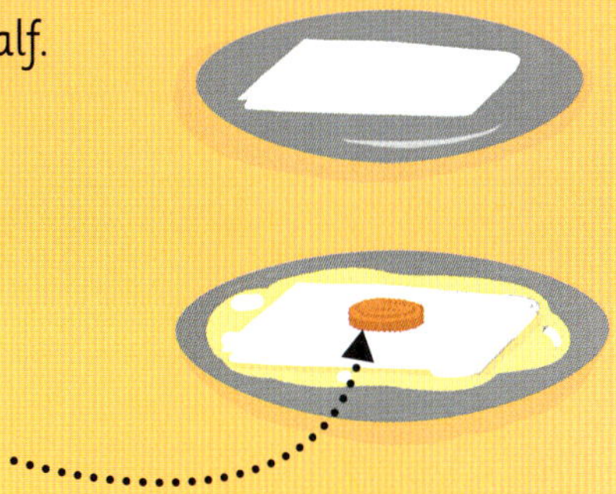

3. Put a penny on top.

4. Keep checking every 20 minutes. What happens?

After one or two hours, the coin starts to go blue-green as the copper reacts with both the air and vinegar.

Do leaves have skeletons?

Yes, they do. You can examine the different parts inside leaves after doing some rubbings.

For each rubbing...

1. Place a leaf under a piece of white paper.
2. Rub a wax crayon over the paper until a picture, like this one, appears...

Many leaves are flat. This helps them to absorb as much sunlight as possible.

The thick line in the middle is the MIDRIB. It makes the leaf sturdy.

These fine lines are VEINS. They carry food and water. Together with the midrib, they support the leaf like a SKELETON.

The stalk that joins a leaf to a plant's stem is known as a PETIOLE.

The skeleton will be all that's left if the rest of an old leaf rots away. You can look out for leaf skeletons under trees.

Make your notes

Compare your rubbings with the leaf above. Can you find the same parts to label?

Make rubbings of different types of leaves, to check which type has the most veins.

Do some leaves have thicker midribs than others?

Why are leaves green?

...Because they contain a green chemical called CHLOROPHYLL. Here are two ways to extract this chemical from some grass cuttings and fresh spinach.

Grass green

1. Cut a handful of fresh grass into pieces. Put them inside a folded piece of paper. 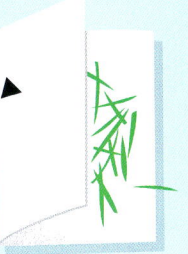
2. Rub it firmly with the back of a spoon. 
3. Open the paper and remove the grass. Look for green marks. If you can't see any, do it again.

The marks are made by chlorophyll.

Spinach green

1. Tear up a handful of spinach leaves into a bowl. 
2. Pour over half a small cup of hot water. Leave for five minutes.
3. Mash the spinach with a fork. 
4. Then tip the contents into a sieve over a second bowl.

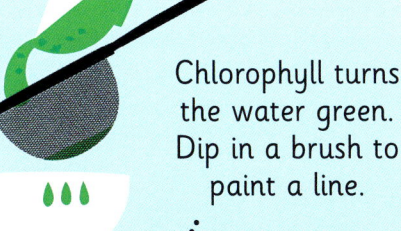

Chlorophyll turns the water green. Dip in a brush to paint a line.

Why do leaves have chlorophyll?

Chlorophyll absorbs sunlight to make food by a process called PHOTOSYNTHESIS. Plants couldn't grow without it.

How do insects walk on water?

Some types of insects skate on top of ponds without sinking. You'll understand how they do it after these experiments.

Spices on the surface

1. Fill a bowl with water and then sprinkle a pinch of dried spices on top.

   Use curry powder, ground pepper or dried chilli flakes.

2. See what happens if you stir the water...

   They're sinking!

3. Start again. This time, drip a little liquid soap onto the water, in the middle. What do the spices do?

Here's what you can't see...

Water is made up of tiny particles. At the surface, they're held together tightly by a FORCE called SURFACE TENSION. So the top of the water is a little like a skin...

Water particle

The spices are light enough to stay on this skin until stirring breaks it up.

Soap breaks the water's skin in a different way...

It pushes away water particles, so the skin moves to the edges of the bowl – taking the spices with it.

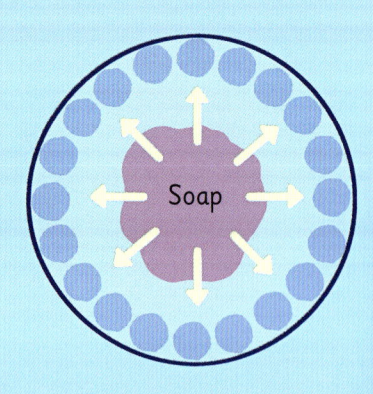

Floating paper clip challenge

1. Fill a bowl with water. Place a paper clip on top. Try to get it to float as many times as you like.

Why can't I do it?

...Because the paper clip keeps piercing the surface.

2. Now rest a small piece of kitchen paper on the water. Gently lay a paper clip on top.

3. Very carefully push the paper down with a fork...

This keeps the paper clip flat, so it DOESN'T break the surface. Now it should float.

What happens if you tip the bowl gently from side to side? Does stirring the water quickly have any effect?

Walking on water

Like the spices and paper clip, these insects can sit on top of water because of surface tension.

Our long legs spread out our weight...

...and tiny hairs on our legs stop them from bursting the surface.

37

The liquid–solid mixture mystery

What happens when you mix something solid with something liquid? Think about these different examples before following the recipe for a mixture that's surprisingly weird...

BAKING
Flour (solid)
+ Water (liquid)
= Dough (solid)

MAKING A DRINK
Milk (liquid)
+ Cocoa powder (solid)
= Hot chocolate (liquid)

PAINTING
Paint block (solid)
+ Water (liquid)
= Paint (liquid, then dries solid)

Could something be liquid then solid again and again?

Weird mixture recipe

1. Pour a cup of cornflour into a bowl.

2. Slowly add half a cup of water.

3. Using your fingers, mix the two together until you CAN'T see any dry lumps.

If it feels VERY runny, add more cornflour.

38

Put your mixture to the test

Tip the bowl slowly from side to side.

Hit the top with the back of a spoon.

Squeeze some mixture in one hand. Does it feel firm?

Roll some mixture between your hands into a ball. Drop it back into the bowl...

How does the mixture move?

Does the spoon sink in or bounce off?

What happens if I open my hand?

How does it land?

Explaining the mystery

Cornflour is a solid made up of lots of tiny particles. They spread out in water, BUT they don't fully DISSOLVE.

DUMMPFF!
Clump   Clump

When you squeeze, hit or roll the mixture, the cornflour particles clump together. That's why it seems SOLID.

If you move the mixture gently or leave it to rest, the particles slide over each other. This makes it look and feel like a LIQUID.

See inside your hand

What happens inside your hand when you bend your fingers? If you make this model, you'll find out.

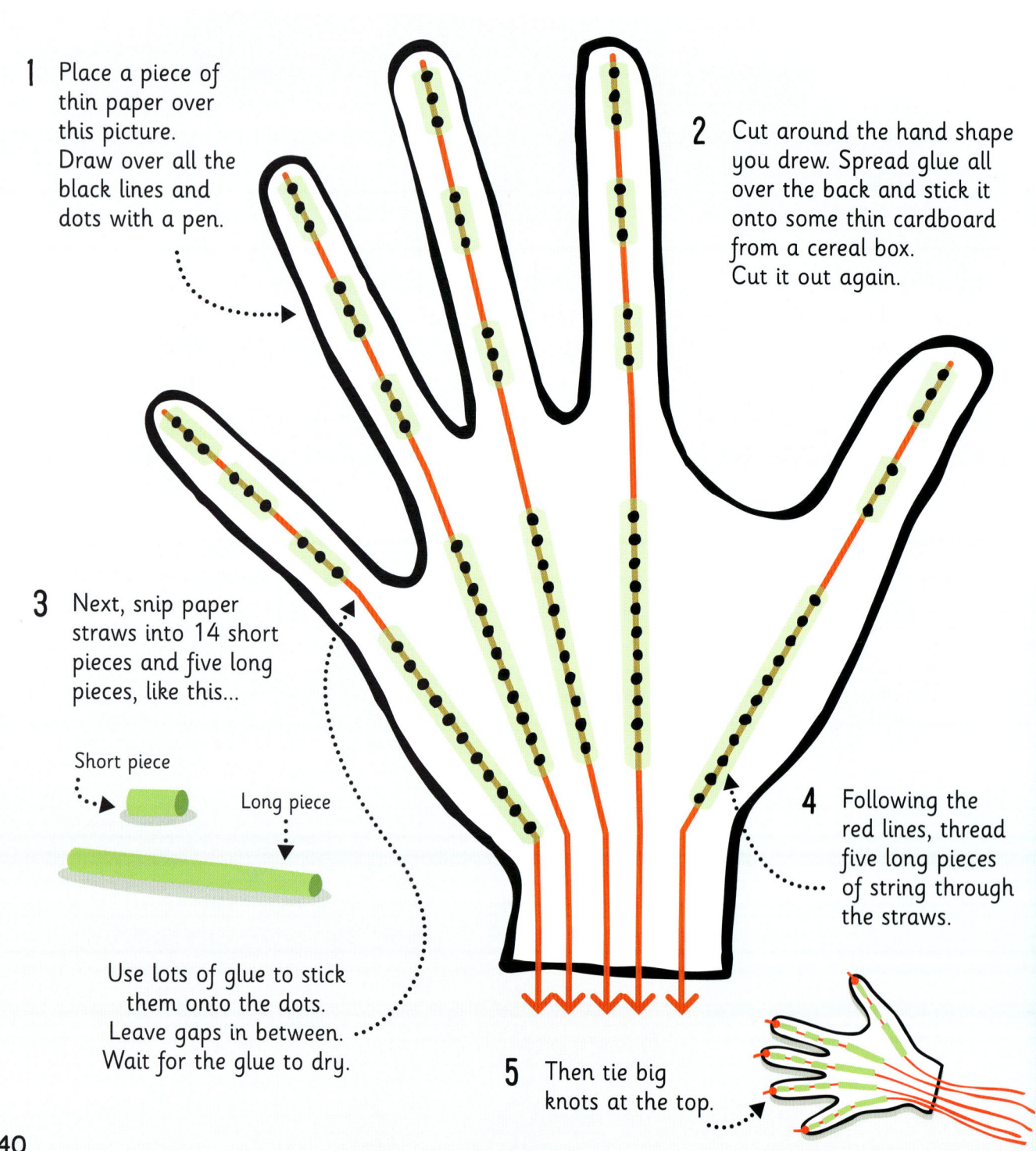

1. Place a piece of thin paper over this picture. Draw over all the black lines and dots with a pen.

2. Cut around the hand shape you drew. Spread glue all over the back and stick it onto some thin cardboard from a cereal box. Cut it out again.

3. Next, snip paper straws into 14 short pieces and five long pieces, like this...

Short piece

Long piece

Use lots of glue to stick them onto the dots. Leave gaps in between. Wait for the glue to dry.

4. Following the red lines, thread five long pieces of string through the straws.

5. Then tie big knots at the top.

40

Test out the model hand

Gently pull on each string, one at a time. What does this do to the fingers and thumb?

I wonder if there are straws and strings in MY hands?

Here's how your hand works...

There are lots of BONES in your hand in the same places as the straws.

Each tendon links to MUSCLES in your arm.

Long, thin TENDONS connect to the bones, a bit like the strings.

When the muscles in your arm PULL your tendons and bones, that makes your fingers bend.

Watch your muscles move

1. Roll up your sleeve. Squeeze your hand into a fist and uncurl your fingers a few times.

   Can you SEE the muscles in your arm moving?

2. Now rest your other hand on your lower arm and try it again...

   I can FEEL my muscles moving!

Why are bubbles round?

Test out this recipe for bubble mix using things you find at home as bubble wands. Go outdoors to blow lots of bubbles and think about how they form.

Bubble mix recipe
1 tablespoon of sugar
2 tablespoons of washing-up liquid
1 cup of water

Carefully mix everything together in a bowl. Keep stirring to dissolve as much sugar as you can.

Which bubble wands are best?

All sorts of things with holes in them make good bubble wands. Dip the ends into the bubble mix and then blow through the holes gently...

Funnels

Paper straws

Slotted spoons

Which wand blows the biggest bubbles?

Cardboard tubes

Cookie cutters

How does blowing turn the liquid into bubbles that float in the air?

First, a stretchy film of soap and water forms across the hole in the wand.

As you blow, the film stretches and traps air inside. This makes a bubble.

The warm air you blew into the bubble is LESS DENSE (see page 20) than the air outside. So the bubble floats for a while.

Won't this bubble be star-shaped?

No! The skin of any bubble always pulls into the shape with the smallest surface area — a sphere. That's because water is made up of tiny particles that want to huddle together as closely as possible.

What made this bubble pop? It wasn't me!

POP!

Water EVAPORATED from the outside of the bubble, making it weak enough to burst.

The sugar in the bubble mix slows this process down. Make the recipe WITHOUT sugar to check if the bubbles pop more quickly.

Can you blow bubbles inside bubbles?

1. Using a straw and some bubble mix, blow very gently onto a plate. Stop when you've made a big bubble.

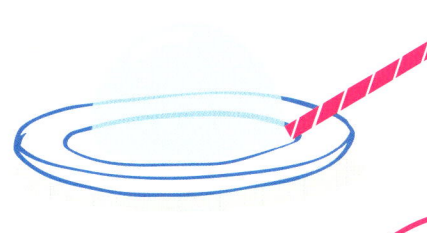

2. First, dip the straw into the bubble mix. Then poke it THROUGH the big bubble and blow another bubble inside. Then pull out the straw carefully.

Why doesn't the first bubble burst?

The first bubble clings to the straw because it's wet from the bubble mix. When you remove the straw, the hole in the bubble snaps shut. What happens if you poke a bubble with a clean, dry straw?

Forcing things to move

All objects stay still unless a big enough FORCE makes them move. Their resistance to start moving is called INERTIA. In these experiments, watch how forces overcome inertia, before turning to page 61 for a full explanation.

Flick a coin

1. Stack at least five coins on top of one another.

2. Use the finger next to your thumb to flick another coin as hard as you can towards the base of the stack.

Does the stack fall over? Repeat this several times to confirm the result. Describe what you see and try to explain what you think is happening.

On the edge

1. Balance a strip of paper over the edge of a table. Stand something the size and weight of a glue stick on top.

2. Slowly tug the strip away from the table. What happens?

3. Set up the experiment again. What do you think will happen if you tug the paper very quickly instead? Give this a try...

Does the tugging force have more of an effect when it's fast or slow?

Tumbling tower

1. Place a piece of card over the top of a wide jug.

2. Stand a cardboard tube on the card. Then balance a lemon on top.

3. Now, quickly hit the card sideways with the back of your hand.

What do you think will happen to the lemon and the tube?

Next steps...

Hold the tube and lemon — how heavy do they feel? Does their weight seem to affect which way they fall?

Then use a light ball of scrunched up paper instead of the lemon.

Does it fall in a different way?

Mixing colours without a brush

Use the scientific properties of water and kitchen paper to mix two colours together. Just follow these steps...

1. Half-fill two glasses with water. Stir in food dyes to turn them different colours.

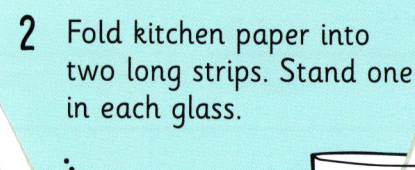

2. Fold kitchen paper into two long strips. Stand one in each glass.

3. Bend both strips into a third glass that's empty. Wait for 30 minutes. Then check what's changed.

0 minutes

30 minutes

Ooooh!

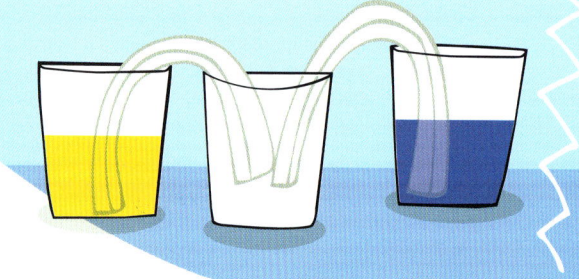

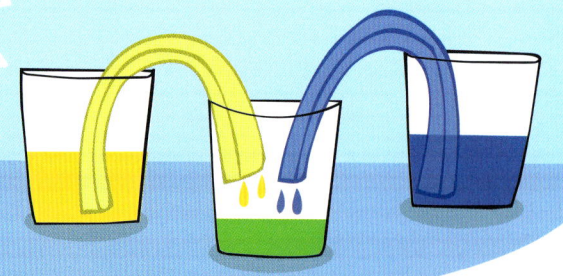

How did it happen?

Kitchen paper absorbs water and dye well. ········▶ After soaking the paper, the dyed waters drip into the empty glass. ········▶ So both mix together into a different colour. No need for a paintbrush!

The colours hiding in your pens

Ink in some felt-tip pens is made up of different colours you CAN'T see. But you can split them apart with this experiment.

1. Cut kitchen paper into short strips.

2. Use different colour pens to draw a thick line above the bottom of each strip.

Black, purple, orange and brown pens often separate well.

3. Dip each strip into water for 30 seconds, keeping the line above the surface. Then leave it to dry. Watch what happens next.

I only used three pens... How did so many colours appear?

The inks DISSOLVE on wet paper and any colours they contain spread out at different speeds. That's why they separate.

The secrets of taste

If you have a cold and your nose feels blocked, you might notice that the things you eat taste strange. On these pages, you can investigate why this happens – and what else affects your SENSE of taste.

Scrumptious!

It doesn't really taste of anything to me.

Test your nose

You'll need two small pieces of apple...

1. Eat one piece while pinching your nose shut. 
2. Let go of your nose before eating the next piece.

Does the taste change?

Now confuse it...

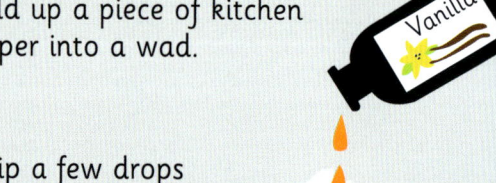

1. Fold up a piece of kitchen paper into a wad.
2. Drip a few drops of vanilla extract onto the wad.
3. Hold it near your nose while you eat another small piece of apple.

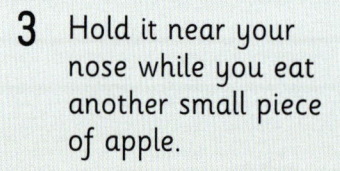

What flavour can you taste?

What's going on?

Your mouth can only detect simple tastes, such as sweet and sour. For complicated flavours, you need your sense of smell, too...

Chewing food releases chemicals.

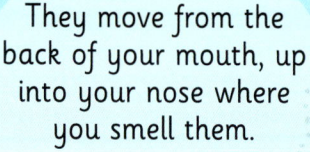

They move from the back of your mouth, up into your nose where you smell them.

The chemicals CAN'T reach your nose when it's pinched or blocked.

Vanilla chemicals are very strong. They go into your nose and overpower the apple in your mouth.

I'm a vanilla pod!

Do you taste with your eyes?

Test a group of people to see how much they rely on what they see when they eat. Set up the experiment beforehand – and keep what you've done secret.

1. Put some vanilla yogurt into three bowls. Add food dyes to turn each one a different colour.

2. Write words for flavours onto eight strips of paper.

Strawberry Lemon Apricot Raspberry Banana Mango Vanilla Blackcurrant

3. Now ask the group to taste each bowl of yogurt and pick the strip that describes its flavour.

This must be raspberry.

Are you sure?

How many people are tricked by this experiment?

Do you think anyone chooses flavours based on the way the bowls of yogurt look?

Apricot Lemon

That's because your brain makes decisions about the way food should taste – EVEN BEFORE you eat it.

Let machines do the work

Discover how cranes help builders and how wind turbines generate electricity by putting simple machines to the test.

How do cranes lift things?

1. Tie a long piece of string to a potato masher. Lift it up and down. How heavy does it feel?

Double knot

2. Next, put the string over a door handle and pull down instead.

Lifting it feels easier. Why?

The handle acts as a machine called a PULLEY, so you can pull down using your body weight to help lift the masher.

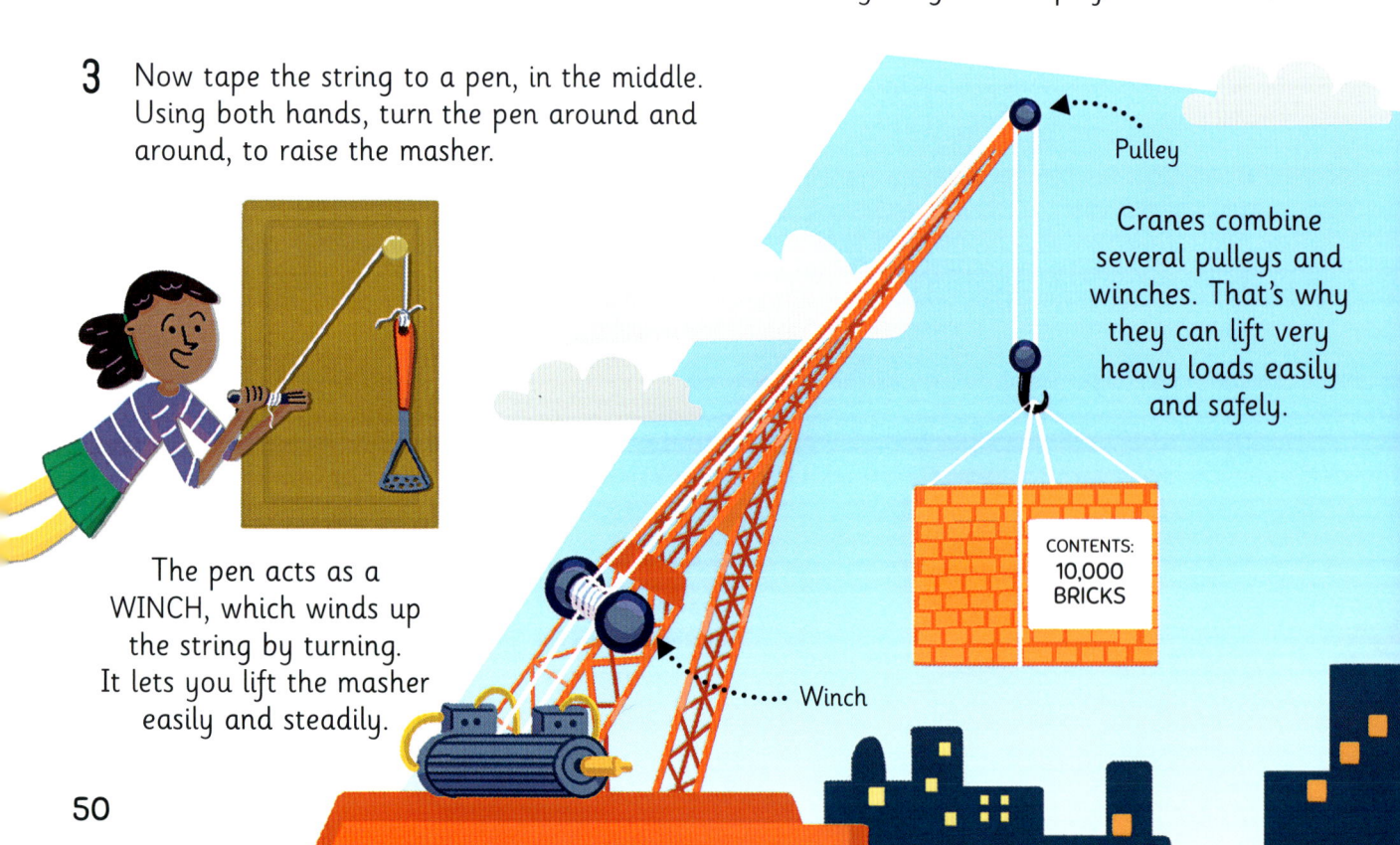

3. Now tape the string to a pen, in the middle. Using both hands, turn the pen around and around, to raise the masher.

The pen acts as a WINCH, which winds up the string by turning. It lets you lift the masher easily and steadily.

Pulley

Cranes combine several pulleys and winches. That's why they can lift very heavy loads easily and safely.

CONTENTS: 10,000 BRICKS

Winch

Why are windy days better for electricity?

1 Fold the top left corner of a piece of paper to the right edge.

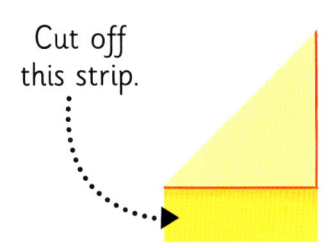

Cut off this strip.

2 Fold the triangle in half. Then open up the paper. Cut from each corner halfway to the middle.

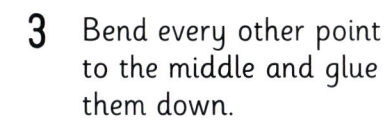

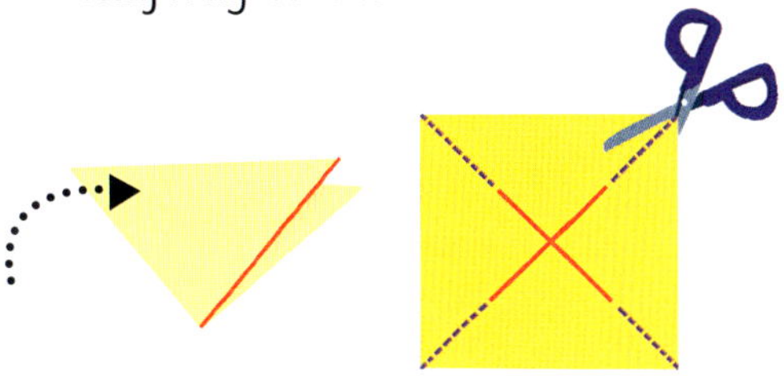

3 Bend every other point to the middle and glue them down.

4 Make a hole in the middle with a pencil. Push through a paper straw, securing it with poster tack.

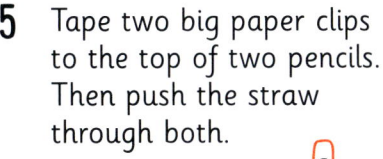

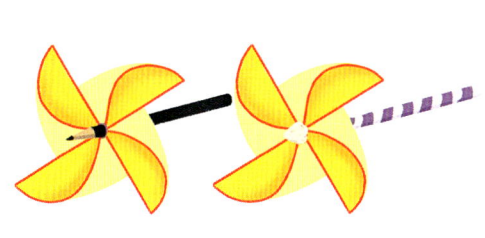

5 Tape two big paper clips to the top of two pencils. Then push the straw through both.

6 Add a pea-sized lump of poster tack to the end of some thread, and tape it to the straw.

7 Holding both pencils, blow on the paper to make it spin.

This kind of machine is a TURBINE. It gives the straw ENERGY to roll up the thread and lift the lump of poster tack. Wind turbines also transform energy, but on a much bigger scale...

First, the wind makes turbines spin with MOVEMENT ENERGY.

Then generators connected to the turbines convert movement energy into ELECTRICAL ENERGY.

Turbine

Generator

Electricity

So, the more the wind blows, the more the turbines turn — and the more electricity is generated.

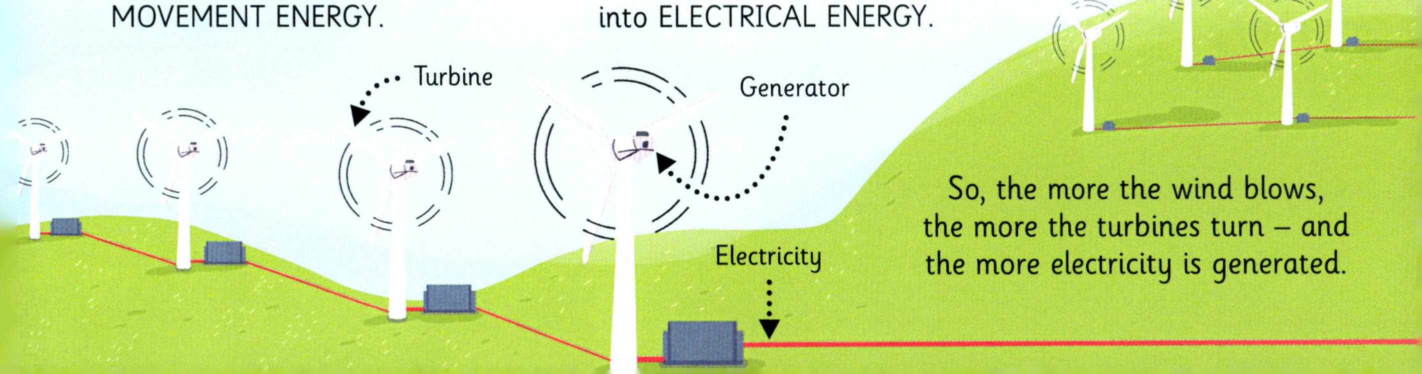

How big is an iceberg?

Icebergs are giant blocks of ice that float in the Arctic and around Antarctica. But how much ice is actually hidden underwater? If you make your own mini iceberg, you can find out.

1 Fill a large yogurt pot with water. Draw a line to mark the height of the water.

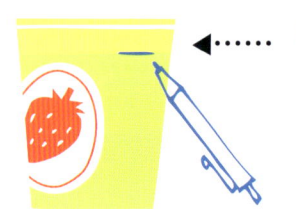

Leave a gap at the top.

2 Leave the pot in a freezer overnight. Then check the height again...

Why is the ice taller?

As water freezes, the particles inside it spread apart, so the ice takes up MORE space.

3 Hold the pot under running water until the ice slides out. Put it on its side and measure its height.

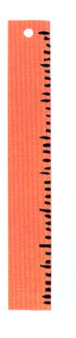

4 Float your iceberg in a bowl of water. Then measure the height of the ice that sticks out.

Do you notice any fizzing?

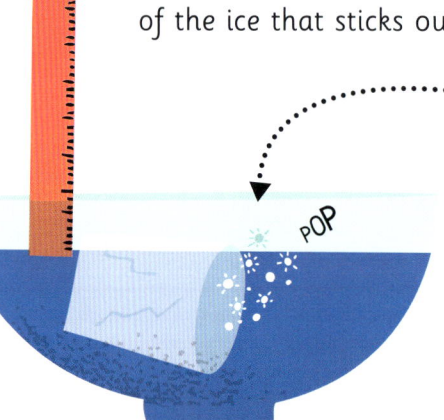

POP

As the ice melts, tiny bubbles of air trapped inside escape.

This happens to real icebergs, too.

5 How many times taller is the part underwater? To calculate this, take away the number you measured in step 4 from the number you measured in step 3. Then divide the answer by the number from step 4.

Aha!

About 90% of all the ice in icebergs is below the water. They're EVEN bigger than they appear.

Why don't seals freeze?

Seals swim for hours on end in ice-cold seas.
So how do they stay warm?

It doesn't feel cold to me...

This experiment will show you why.

1. Reuse a bag from some food packaging. Put a spoon of fat, such as soft butter or lard, inside.

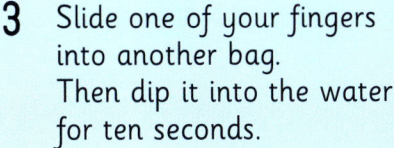

2. Fill a bowl with cold water and some ice cubes.

3. Slide one of your fingers into another bag. Then dip it into the water for ten seconds.

How cold does it feel?

4. Keep the bag on your finger as you poke it into the bag of fat. Squish it around your finger before testing the water again.

Does the water feel the same as before?

Trapping body heat

The bag on its own CAN'T STOP heat escaping from your finger, so it soon feels cold. BUT heat doesn't travel through fat easily, so it keeps your finger warm.

We have a thick layer of fat called BLUBBER under our skin. That's what traps our body heat.

What makes things balance?

With these experiments you can investigate how things stay upright without toppling over.

Woah!

Wobbling tubes

1. Roll thick paper into a long tube. Tape down the edge.

2. Make two more tubes from smaller pieces of paper.

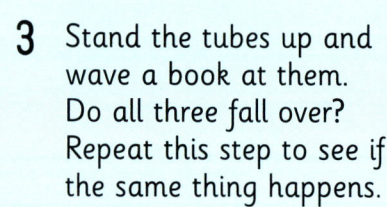

3. Stand the tubes up and wave a book at them. Do all three fall over? Repeat this step to see if the same thing happens.

Why is the short tube so steady?

It's to do with its BALANCING POINT.

That's an imaginary point in the middle of ANY object around which its weight balances.

A tube stays upright so long as the balancing point is directly above its base.

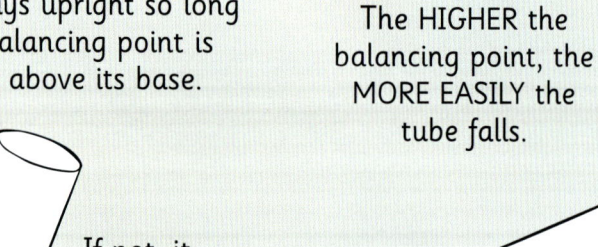

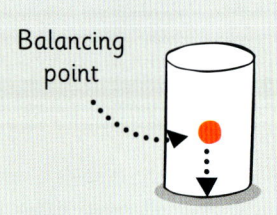

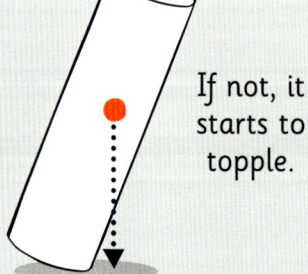

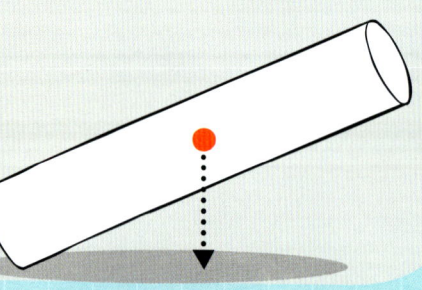

The HIGHER the balancing point, the MORE EASILY the tube falls.

Balancing point

If not, it starts to topple.

Tilting can

1. Tilt an empty drinks can and try balancing it. Does this work?

2. Add some water to the can so it's about a third full. Then try to balance it again...

You need the weight of the water to LOWER the can's balancing point. Then it can tilt without falling over.

Balancing forks trick

1. Firmly slot together the prongs of a pair of forks, like this...

2. Push a cocktail stick through the middle of both forks.

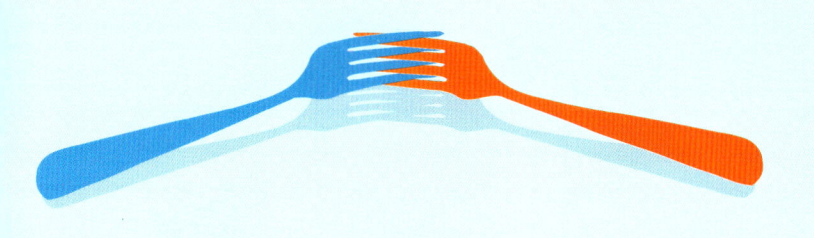

3. Rest the stick on the rim of a tall glass, checking the picture on the right. Carefully move the stick and forks together until they all balance.

This step might take a little while. Keep trying!

The forks and stick SHARE a balancing point in the SPACE between them.

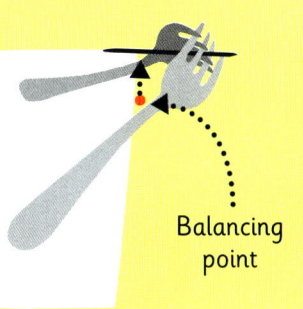

Balancing point

The stick won't fall off if it rests on the rim above the point.

How is butter made?

If you look at the ingredients on a packet of dairy butter, you'll see that the first one is usually cream. So what turns it into butter?

I thought cream was runny...

1. Half-fill a clean jar with double cream. Screw on the lid. Leave it out of the fridge for 30 minutes.

This experiment is harder to do if the cream is very cold.

2. Shake the jar as hard as you can for about five minutes. This takes effort!

Keep shaking even if the cream doesn't seem to be moving.

3. Stop when you hear a thumping sound and see lots of thin liquid.

4. Empty the jar into a sieve over a bowl.

This liquid is called buttermilk. You can drink it – or pour it over cereal.

This solid lump is butter.

5. Put the butter into a clean bowl of cold water. Press the butter several times with the back of a spoon.

The water will turn cloudy.

56

6 Tip away the water using the sieve to catch the butter. Then repeat step 5 until the water stays clear.

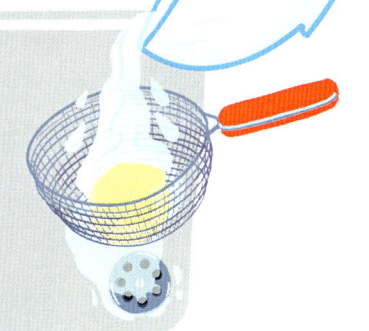

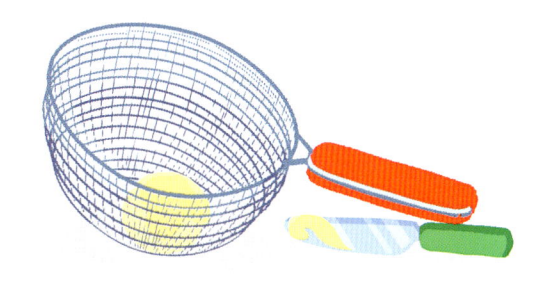

7 Use the sieve to drain the butter. It's now ready to spread on bread and taste.

Store the butter in the fridge and eat it within a few days.

Yum! Where did the cream go?

From cream to butter

1 Cream is made up of lots of tiny blobs of fat, or GLOBULES, in a milky liquid.

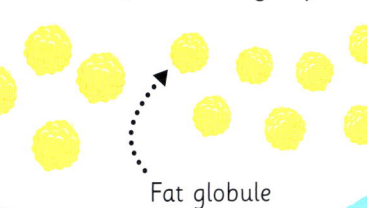

Fat globule

2 When you shake the cream, the globules smash into each other and cling together around bubbles of air.

Air bubble

That's why the cream gets thicker.

3 More and more globules cling together as you shake. At last, they clump into butter.

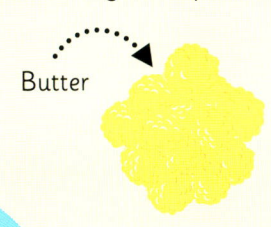

Butter

As butter forms, it pushes out liquid buttermilk.

4 Any drops of buttermilk stuck inside the butter are pressed out by the spoon.

The BUTTERMILK mixes with water making it cloudy.

But BUTTER and water DON'T mix.

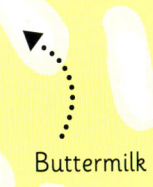

Buttermilk

Where do clouds come from?

Clouds are made up of tiny, floating droplets of water. This page will show you where the droplets come from.

Vanishing puddle

1. On a sunny day, tip some water onto a hard path outdoors to make a puddle.
2. Draw around its edge with a piece of chalk. 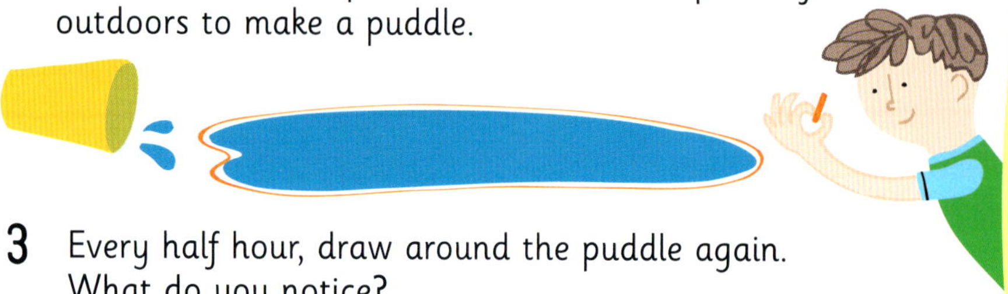
3. Every half hour, draw around the puddle again. What do you notice?

It's shrinking!

Why it vanishes

Heat from the Sun turns the puddle into WATER VAPOUR. It's made up of invisible particles that spread into the air above. This process is called EVAPORATION. It happens to the surface of rivers, lakes and oceans all around the world.

To find out what happens as the vapour rises, try the experiment below.

Mystery droplets

1. Half-fill a jar with hot water.
2. Turn the lid upside down and place it on top of the jar. Then add a couple of ice cubes. 
3. After a few minutes, lift up the lid and touch it underneath.

It feels wet.

Why it's wet

First, some of the hot water turns into vapour. But when it reaches the cold lid, the vapour turns BACK into liquid water. This process is called CONDENSATION.

High up in the sky, something similar is going on. The air is very cold, so it CONDENSES the rising vapour into droplets, making clouds.

As more droplets cluster together, they become too heavy to float. That's why they start to fall as rain.

Answers

8–9 What's shocking about static?

GLUE-FREE STICKING
Static flows away from the ruler when you tap it onto metal. So the paper stops clinging to the ruler.

BENDING WATER
Static isn't strong enough to bend fast-flowing water.

Ahh!

10–11 The look of the Moon

SHAPE-SHIFTING MOON
The shadow on the orange grows bigger and smaller. When your back is to the light, you won't be able to see the shadow.

WHY THE MOON IS SPOTTY
The heavier the marble and the further it falls, the bigger the crater it makes.

16 Why do bread and cakes rise?

SODA POWER
When cake mixture is baked in a hot oven, the bicarbonate of soda releases bubbles of carbon dioxide. This makes the cake rise and its texture light and fluffy.

17 Bicarbonate of soda + acid = ?

The reaction stops after a minute or so. If you add more bicarbonate of soda, vinegar or lemon juice, the mixture will fizz again.

20 The egg that floats and sinks

Old eggs sometimes float in water WITHOUT any salt. That's because the egg inside the shell releases gases as it goes bad.

WHAT DOES DENSER MEAN?
A coin feels much denser than a piece of dried pasta.

NEXT STEPS
Flour DOESN'T dissolve in water, so it CAN'T make it any denser. That's why the egg still sinks.
A pebble is very dense, so salt can't make the water dense enough for it to float.

21 Dancing raisins

EXPAND THE EXPERIMENT
As the bubbles in sparkling water burst, the water becomes less fizzy. Eventually, there are too few bubbles to make the raisins dance.
The water gets sweeter because raisins contain sugar. As they dance, some sugar mixes into the water.
Bubbles can't cling to smooth lentils, so they won't dance.

22 Can you see sounds?

JUMPING SALT
Hitting the tray harder makes the sound vibrations bigger, so the salt jumps more.

23 Catching a whisper

NOW TEST IT OUT…
Keeping the string straight and tight helps sound vibrations to travel along it. If the string touches another surface, the vibrations are absorbed before they reach the cup.

24–25 How do planes fly?

The way you fold or throw a paper plane can affect the way it flies. So don't worry if your results don't match the ones below.

If you throw your plane upside down, it usually flies upside down, too.

NOSE CLIP
The extra weight makes the plane fly straight before falling nose first.

FLIGHT ANGLE
Tilting up: the plane flies in a big curve.
Tilting down: the plane flies towards the ground.

WING TIPS
Both up: the plane flies far and straight.
Both down: the plane glides smoothly.
One up one down: the plane wobbles.
Only one up: the plane spins to the side.

FOIL PLANES AND MORE
Magazine paper is easy to fold. Foil planes fly well but they're fiddly to fold and they can get crushed. Cardboard is too thick to fold neatly, and it's too heavy for planes to fly well. Newspaper jumbo jets fly more slowly. If you manage to fold a paper plane from a rectangle about 4cm (1.5 inches) long, then it will fly but it might shake.

28–29 Playing with air pressure

KEEPING AN UPSIDE-DOWN GLASS FULL
Tugging the card breaks the seal. This allows gravity to pull the water down.

RAISING THE LEVEL
You see bubbles in step 1 because air rises to the surface from the jar. When you lift the jar above the surface, the water flows into the bowl because of gravity.

32–33 Transforming pennies

IDENTIFYING ACIDS
Oil doesn't contain acid. There is a small amount of acid in milk. Both cola and lemon juice are very acidic.

34 Do leaves have skeletons?

MAKE YOUR NOTES
Leaves have different numbers and patterns of veins – as well as midribs of different widths and lengths.

36–37 How do insects walk on water?

FLOATING PAPER CLIP CHALLENGE
Tipping the bowl gently WON'T break the surface, so the paper clip keeps floating. But if you stir the water, you break the surface tension and sink the paper clip.

38–39 The liquid-solid mixture mystery

PUT YOUR MIXTURE TO THE TEST
When you tip the bowl, the mixture flows to the side.
The spoon bounces off the surface. Before opening your hand, the mixture feels firm. But it then becomes runny and drips between your fingers.
The ball becomes liquid and disappears into the rest of the mixture.

40–41 See inside your hand

TEST OUT THE MODEL HAND
Pulling each string makes the finger or thumb it's connected to move.

The little finger is bending.

42–43 Why are bubbles round?

WHICH BUBBLE WANDS ARE BEST?
It's harder to blow air through bubble wands with bigger holes, but they do make bigger bubbles.

CAN YOU BLOW BUBBLES INSIDE BUBBLES?
A bubble bursts if you poke it with a dry straw.

POP!

44–45 Forcing things to move

FLICK A COIN
The force of the flicked coin pushes out the bottom coin in the stack only. That's because the other coins have enough inertia to resist moving.

ON THE EDGE
The glue stick stays in place when you tug the paper quickly. But tugging the paper slowly overcomes the glue stick's inertia, so it falls over.

TUMBLING TOWER
Only the tube is knocked sideways with the piece of card. The lemon falls straight down into the jug. This is because the lemon is heavier and has more inertia. But a ball of paper will fall out to the side along with the tube and card.

48–49 The secrets of taste

TEST YOUR NOSE
The apple won't taste of much when you pinch your nose.

NOW CONFUSE IT...
The apple will taste of vanilla.

Science words

This page explains some of the words used in this book. Words shown in **bold** have their own entries.

ACID A **chemical** that reacts with many materials.

AIR PRESSURE The **force** of air pushing against a surface.

AIR RESISTANCE The **force** pushing against an object as it moves through the air.

ASTEROID A rocky object in space.

BLUBBER A thick layer of fat under the skin of seals and whales.

CARBON DIOXIDE A **gas**. It makes drinks fizzy.

CHEMICAL A substance that **reacts** with other substances or one that's made when other substances **react**.

CHLOROPHYLL A green **chemical** found in plants.

CONDENSE To change from a **gas** into a **liquid**.

DENSE How heavy something feels compared to its size.

DISSOLVE To break up into tiny parts that mix evenly in a **liquid**.

ENERGY The power that makes things work.

EVAPORATE To change from a **liquid** into a **gas**.

FORCE A push or pull or bend or twist that makes things move or change shape.

FOSSIL The remains of ancient living things.

GAS A substance that can change shape and fill any space.

GLOBULE A small, round **particle**.

GRAVITY The **force** that pulls everything down to Earth.

ICEBERG A floating block of frozen freshwater.

INERTIA The tendency of an object to stay still until a **force** makes it move.

LIQUID A substance that can change shape but can't take up more or less space.

METAL A material that's usually shiny and hard.

MIXTURE Two or more substances mixed together.

MUSCLE Part of the body that makes other body parts move.

OXYGEN A **gas** in the air.

PARTICLE A very tiny part.

PHOTOSYNTHESIS The process that uses **energy** from sunlight to make food for plants.

PULLEY A machine that changes the direction of a pulling **force**.

REACT To change.

REFRACTION The bending of light as it passes through different substances.

SENSE People have five basic senses: taste, sight, smell, hearing and touch.

SOLID A substance that keeps its shape and can't spread out.

STATIC An electric charge made when materials rub together.

SURFACE TENSION The **force** that holds water **particles** together at the surface.

TURBINE A machine with blades that turn.

VIBRATION A very fast movement backwards and forwards.

WINCH A machine used to wind up cable.

Index

acids, 17, 32, 59, 60, 62
air, 6, 7, 24, 28, 29, 32, 33, 42, 52, 57, 60, 61, 62
air pressure, 28-29, 60, 62
air resistance, 6, 62
asteroids, 11, 62

balancing, 54-55
bicarbonate of soda, 16, 17, 59
blubber, 53, 62
bones, 41
brain, 19, 30, 31, 49
bread, 16
bubbles, 16, 17, 21, 29, 42-43, 52, 57, 59, 60, 61
butter, 56-57

cakes, 16, 59
carbon dioxide, 16, 17, 21, 59, 62
chemicals, 32, 33, 35, 48, 62
chlorophyll, 35, 62
clouds, 58
colours, 30, 46, 47
condensing, 58, 62
copper, 32, 33
cranes, 50
craters, 11, 59

dense, 20, 21, 42, 59, 62
dinosaurs, 26, 27
dissolving, 20, 39, 47, 59, 62

Earth, the, 10, 12
eating, 48
electricity, 8, 9, 51
energy, 51, 62
evaporating, 27, 43, 58, 62
eyes, 15, 30, 49

fat, 53, 57, 62
fingers, 40-41, 53, 61
flavours, 48-49
floating, 20, 21, 36, 37, 42, 52, 59, 60
flying, 24-25, 60
food dye, 46, 49
forces, 6, 24, 28, 29, 36, 44-45, 61, 62
fossils, 26-27, 62
freezing, 52, 53

gas, 16, 21, 33, 59, 62
globules, 57, 62
gravity, 6, 24, 28, 60, 62

hands, 40-41, 61
hearing, 23
heat, 53

ice, 12, 13, 52, 53, 58
icebergs, 52, 62
inertia, 44-45, 61, 62
ink, 47
insects, 36, 37, 60

leaves, 6, 34, 35, 60
lift, 24
lifting, 50
light, 10, 15
liquid, 32, 38, 39, 58, 61, 62

machines, 50, 51
memory, 18-19
metal, 8, 32, 33, 62
mixtures, 16, 17, 38, 39, 42, 46, 57, 61, 62
Moon, the, 10-11, 59
mouth, 48
muscles, 41, 62

nose, 48, 61

optical illusions, 30-31
oxygen, 32, 62

paper planes, 24-25, 60
parachutes, 6
particles, 20, 28, 36, 39, 43, 52, 62
pennies, 32-33
photosynthesis, 35, 62
plants, 35
pulleys, 50, 62

rain, 58
reacting, 17, 32, 33, 62
refraction, 15, 62

salt, 20, 22
seals, 53
seas, 12-13, 52, 53, 58
seeds, 7
seeing, 14-15, 22, 30-31
senses, 48, 49, 62
shadows, 10, 59
sinking, 20, 21, 36, 37, 59, 60
smelling, 48
soap, 36, 42
solid, 38, 39, 61, 62
sound, 22, 23, 59, 60
static electricity, 8-9, 59, 62
sugar, 43

Sun, the, 10, 58
sunlight, 34, 35
surface tension, 36-37, 60, 62

taste, 21, 48-49, 61
tendons, 41
trees, 7

vapour, 58
verdigris, 33
vibrations, 22, 23, 59, 60, 62

water, 9, 12, 13, 14, 15, 16, 20, 21, 27, 28, 29, 33, 36, 37, 42, 43, 46, 47, 52, 53, 57, 58, 59, 60
weight, 45, 50, 55, 60, 61
winches, 50, 62
wind turbines, 50, 51, 62

yeast, 16, 59

Now we're SCIENTISTS!

Managing designer:
Stephen Moncrieff

Managing editor:
Jane Chisholm

First published in 2022 by Usborne Publishing Ltd., 83-85 Saffron Hill, London EC1N 8RT, United Kingdom. usborne.com Copyright © 2022 Usborne Publishing Ltd. The name Usborne and the Balloon logo are Trademarks of Usborne Publishing Ltd. All rights reserved. No part of this publication may be reproduced, stored in any retrievable system, or transmitted in any form or by any means, without the prior permission of the publisher. UKE.

Usborne Publishing is not responsible and does not accept liability for the availability or content of any website other than its own, or for any exposure to harmful, offensive or inaccurate material which may appear on the Web. Usborne Publishing will have no liability for any damage or loss caused by viruses that may be downloaded as a result of browsing the sites it recommends.